Spoke the Dark Matter

Sundress Publications • Knoxville, TN

Book Editor: Erin Elizabeth Smith
Managing Editor: Erin Elizabeth Smith and Tennison Black
Editorial Assistant: Kanika Lawton
Editorial Interns: Izzy Astuto, Whitney Cooper, Addie Dodge, Jen Gayda
Gupta, Hedaya Hasan

Colophon: This book is set in Goudy Old Style.

Cover Image: Errol Whittaker

Cover Design: Kristen Ton

Book Design: Erin Elizabeth Smith

Spoke the Dark Matter
Michelle Whittaker

Acknowledgments

Bertrois Magazine: "Freedom from Fear"

Breadcrumbs Magazine: "Frequently Axed Answers" and "The Lovers in the Pine Barren"

Fjords Review: "Partial Life Review" (published as "What It Looks Like") and "Directions for Singing"

Gulf Coast: "Opening" and "Unsound Health"

Maintenant: The Journal of Contemporary Dada Writing and Art: "Dada" (published as "He is He is He is")

PANK Magazine: "Me & Monster"

Plume: "In Preparation for Ascendance"

Poem-A-Day from the Academy of American Poets: "Our Quarantine Story"

Poetrybay: "Fractured"

Provincetown Arts Magazine: "My Dearest Black-billed Streamertail"

Shenandoah: "Bonefish"

The Slowdown Podcast: "My Dearest Black-billed Streamertail"

The Southampton Review: "Practicing Positive Mental Attitude" and "To the Eyes Beholding Stardust"

Upstreet Literary Review: "I Miss You Texting Goodnight" and "On the Last Day of Becoming Us"

"A Quiet Surge of Dystopia" is an essay written for *Long Island Climate Change and Justice Volume* (SUNY Press) prior to the COVID-19 pandemic.

Spoke the Dark Matter was possible with generous support from the NYSCA/NYFA Artist Fellowship Program.

CONTENTS

In Preparation for Ascendance (1976)   11
Opening   12
First Generation Eclipsed   14
A Quiet Surge of Dystopia   15
In Preparation for Ascendance (1993)   17
Frequently Axed Answers   21
Partial Life Review   22
A Quiet Surge of Dystopia   23
Strange & Merciful Days   24
A Quiet Surge of Dystopia   26
My mom jokes about how my teenage scowl ruined family photos   28
A Quiet Surge of Dystopia   29
My Dearest Black-Billed Streamertail   30
The Labor of Counterpoint   32
Unsound Health   35
Fractures   36
A Quiet Surge of Dystopia   38
On the Snowy Shore of Lake Erie   39
Still Life & Half-Turned Lover   41
On the Last Day of Becoming Us   43
A Field Guide for a Positive Mental Attitude   46
A Quiet Surge of Dystopia   49
Me and Monster   50
A Quiet Surge of Dystopia   52
Directions for Singing   54
A Quiet Surge of Dystopia   55
Bonefish   56
The Limitations of Repose   58
Why are you without a Home?   59
Ascending from a Slough   61
A Quiet Surge of Dystopia   65
To the Eyes Beholding Stardust   66
A Quiet Surge of Dystopia   67

Spoke the Ancestral   68
Dada   70
A Quiet Surge of Dystopia   72
Self-Portrait as a Bilateral Night   73
Our Quarantine Story   75
A Warning about Entanglements   76
The Lovers Move to the Pine Barrens   77
Freedom from Fear   79
A Quiet Surge of Dystopia   81
how to cradle a stranger   82
Dear Power, We Possess   83

Notes   85
Thank You   87
About the Author   89

dedicated to george & working artists

your body running off each undesired desired encounter
−Claudia Rankine

In Preparation for Ascendance
for J

Consider Kingston, Jamaica, 1976.
Notice in the photo how your mother
in a mini skirt, body spiking as a Royal palm,
is three months pregnant & not smiling.

Notice where she looks, as if refocusing
a revelation not referenced into a restraint,
while a few miles away, political parties riot
with their flintlock triggers & ratchet knives.

Now consider being shown how the arugula
has gone to seed in front of your city
rental decades later, note how their petals
have crossed the broken police barricade.

Then look again at your beautiful mother
squinting beyond the frame at plumes rising
as a nimbus cloud shaped like the United States.

See how the keyhole burns?

Opening

after Philip Glass

Glass, as ambitious as double consciousness
handles the business of paranoia, handles
the notion of a blue heaven rotting at the canopies.

Opening Glass is good for tuning the volume,
every nine minutes when the landlords bicker
or yell hellish rants as you place a brown ear

to their pipes, decoding smash & cuts, questioning:
Should I call for help? Should I respond to faint cries
behind the fridge where the wasps hold up?

Opening Glass is good for the quick jump
of what sounded like a gunshot— or a shotgun
for you cannot quite identify a body

larger-than-a-raccoon or smaller-than-a-deer
deadening at the side of the yard.

Let us pray

Imagine "Opening" Glass
as a coroner at the edge of our mascara,

conducting scene notes about the tumbling sky:
We know it was not a bird or a drone or a plane.

It was not Superman or Ororo "Storm" Munroe.
It was not caped or cotton-wearing or spandexing.

We know it was not a savior of any kind.
It was not uniformed or unifying

as a dad or a granddad or an older sibling,
but streaming unscripted toward

this polyphonic Earth
where there's no one who exists to save us.

First Generation Eclipsed

Sometimes the desire to identify yourself
severs the respiratory tract of a catfish

that's lemon-scented, like how my unfavorable
political ambivalence rising inside me discards

anger for a robust spiked tea. Similarly, whenever
I was sick with elegies, my mother made me drink

boiled garlic until I vomited. But either way,
I suppose a good purge is necessary for arriving

at the blustering truth that conflict itself is a nemesis.
But should I really deny the gutted ensemble

as ironic on my cutting board? Or consider *this*
as post-process inner work, reflecting a proverbial

fight about who on this earth *is* an immaculate pioneer,
when thinking of the blood moon composing its hold?

A Quiet Surge of Dystopia

You were surrounded by resplendent pitch pine barrens, a string of mom &
pop shops, a movie theater, a Handy Pantry, local farms, rocky northern
beaches. This was 1980, Long Island, when your neighborhood was
somewhat racially and culturally diverse. Over time, the waning greenery
shifted into a nostalgic dream, like a loose rendition of your Roman Catholic
gaze, reminiscent of dense fern gully hills crowning the Spanish roads of
Jamaica, from where your parents emigrated before becoming American
citizens. Even in the 90s, when you watched vacant front lawns turn brown
while families you grew to love were displaced by homogenous
homeownerships who floated white boats and monster-tire trucks as the new
garden view, this was still *your* island.

And when we entered the millennium, the grand acres of forest at the dead-end of the lane were swiftly chopped by contractors, as you congregated with the last of your childhood friends on banana bikes to watch the tragic felling. The new vinyl-siding houses stood proud like hybrid flowers. For some reason, they reminded you of how Dad made you and your siblings uproot the dandelions from the manicured woodchip footpaths around your house every weekend. You always felt a vague guilt about murdering them. *Years later, you learned that the presence of weeds teaches us which nutrients are missing from the soil.*

In Preparation for Ascendance
Kingston, Jamaica, 1993

On Heywood Street stringy mangoes were spoiled.
Horseflies and mosquitos spurred at our ankles.

Fruit flies protected what was theirs
as we rummaged through the soursop.

Granma haggled with higglers for oxtail & saltfish
as elders grabbed my hands, naming me *granddaughta.*

Some girls my age sat with their mothers,
slumped in corners, or soured against walls,

inching their preteen shoulders from side-to-side
like anancies alongside the stonework.

Sleep snaked in the eyes of fussy babies
too exhausted by the humidity to cry.

Most days, the heat was insufferable,
despite the shade of our slim visors.

*

In the market square, the *men dem*
constantly grabbed my upper arms,

held my wrists and harassed my hips,
when Granma stepped away to haggle.

Pretty & *gal* & *pickney* grew as enemies inside me.

Sometimes she'd turn around and scold them,
sounding off her alarming gold bangles.

A wha do dem man yah, Cha! Granma exclaimed.
But they had already left their marks.

No amount of sea bathing or mineral baths
could rid me of their touch.

Nakedness and bathing suits made me
as nauseous as when I ate escovitch

fish and cornmeal "festival" at Hellshire Beach.
Often, I sat toilet-sick in the bathroom,

needing a wash-out, as my father would say.
He was right in that I wanted purification.

So I wore the same baggie black shirt and shorts
even though Granma would complain:

A wha mek yu wear so much black,
wen wi Jamaicans such colorful people?

*

Granma pointed to the stretch marks
on my brown calves and said *men dem*

might not want to marry me.
They would think I already had children.

*

When we finally arrived home from the market,
I noticed a long gray hair on my forearm.

After Granma inspected the carelessness of its color
she said, *no, nuh pluck it, or yu gwan get bad luck.*

I asked her *why* as I followed her into the yard.

She grabbed at an ackee on a tree
and hissed through her teeth—*dem nuh ripe*

—*it wi kill yu* if harvested too soon.

Frequently Axed Answers

The thought of my Granma's death often visits
the thought of Jesus cleaned and prepared for gravity.

My oncologist outlines a group of disorganized nodules
that mirror the grassplots of a Bahamian graveyard.

The thought of baking soda laced with lead interrupts
day drinking & night drinking masks ovarian grief.

The reality of being born again crawls in and out of bed,
and certain positions seem prone to restless griping.

Loving someone depressed, dying, & in self-denial,
deepens the daily routine for creating art like grievances

circling her courtyard in front of geraniums
also diseased, as if deeming ourselves mapless or ageless

or like a luminary acquiescence
or just tormented when virtue subsumes the blade —

Partial Life Review
after Marie Howe

It was like the moment when a rare pine warbler flew over the highway lane
just before entering those shelf clouds in the near distance,
just before you saw the wall of rain leaving inches of itself further down
the road before hydro-planking disturbances. But for a moment
you felt this deluge as a divine sanction or sweet suspicion
like the over-arousal of when a hatchback's tires and brakes disagree
as a steering committee, or very much like when you kept checking
for the headlights in your rearview mirror, when for a moment
you are offered clarity about why your partner paints bamboo shoots
over and over, and why you don't have the heart to answer
when asked again if this time it looks like the real thing:
when no, the nature of it looks to me like cancer.

A Quiet Surge of Dystopia

You tolerated the lack of amenities for multiple seasons, under the hearsay assumption that many people in the area must have experienced similar or far worse living conditions. One night when you couldn't sleep, you watched the condensation from your breath wisp in front of your face and thought of how, at a local party, someone said with the straightest, apathetic face that *there are no homeless people on Long Island.* The next day, your neighbor showed you the brown water coming out of her sink faucet. She was also a person of color, who lived there for years, *but didn't want to cause any trouble.*

Strange & Merciful Days

When I ran out of whole food
I ate from cans of albacore
& skipjack
to afford my gyno appointments
with a nurse practitioner
 & shiny medical instruments.

Before and after my biopsy, I considered
bashing tambourines for insurance money.

After the anesthesiologist asked me
to count myself away
inside my bedhead,
the cervical view
waltzed out
& dropped dead.
God also dropped dead
after the last Seraphim forgot
        my request & toppled.

Then entered a thunder
beholding me awake again,

& like when gossip

echoes in the corridor's archways,

the anesthesiologist asked me

to count 18,000 dollars away.

At a cursory glance, I thought

I understood what it meant

to lose black magic.

Lovers and friends were half-right

to read my unresponsiveness as prolonged grief,

but I didn't want to appear defensive.

I saw ambivalence more like witnessing

the last cardinal of the season

capturing the Bella moth

against the nectar in the moss.

A Quiet Surge of Dystopia

Saddled with student debt, commuting between three jobs, your lifestyle was that of an art-obsessed, quasi-complacent, emissions-producing, scarcity-mindset. Your various rental situations ranged from wolf-spider infested rooms, waterlogged converted garages, and brick-layered studios piping in rust-brown water. The worst apartments had broken heat during the winter months. *Cold was as cold as a stiff neck with a cold virus that would take you months to recover when it should have taken weeks.*

You kept telling yourself existential dread was normal. Unexpected upsets were normal. Weekly power outages were normal. And the flooding of your one-room apartment after every passing storm crept into normalcy, as your electric upright piano grew accustomed to sitting in an inch or two of saltwater. Eventually, hyper-normalization would have your livelihood near the achilles. You became mindful that keeping your living place safe and sealed off from the natural elements solely depended on the landlord honoring the human lease.

My mom jokes about how my teenage scowl ruined family photos

After I sigh,
my partner agrees
I should learn
to vacation,

but our view does look
like a landslide depression
although I know it's a shoal
during low tide.

I open a broken porch gate
between my lips
and after a few snapshots,
latch it all behind.

A Quiet Surge of Dystopia

Friends would ask why you stayed in subpar apartments when your requests for repairs were ignored—and you replied that it was what you could afford on your own. You understood many of these friends were married or lived with parents or left the island. They asked why you didn't report these violations, since it's against the law to deny tenants clean water and heat. You were embarrassed and defensive at such questionings, not wanting to explain you were afraid of becoming homeless and privately thought you must've had a fracture in your self-worth. When you looked for new places to live, potential landlords would be so kind on the phone until they saw your brown epidermis step out of the car. You retraced your parents' stories about how their realtor in late 70's would only take them to towns on one side of the railroad tracks where other Black people lived, which was okay, but your Dad wanted a house in an area his coworkers suggested. Evidentially, they provided testimony to a housing authority for investigations into discrimination practices on the island—and won.

My Dearest Black-Billed Streamertail

Apparently, we have chosen
to spend our lives in semi-solitude,

studying the intimacies
of caverns and coastlines.

Years ago, *The Daily Gleaner* remarked
how the Arawaks called you a warrior god,

but my Auntie calls you a 'doctor'
with a photographic memory.

I wonder which you would prefer to be,
craving nectar as much as you need water.

I can imagine why my ancestors plucked away
your emerald feathers from the flank of your body,

even as I hold my compulsion to my chest
like a fist crumpling an unsent love letter.

Instead, these hands brim with gratitude,
shredding black tupelo leaves into compost

readying for the season where the bluebonnets
bring forth narrow spikes of light.

Don't we crave conversation
as much as we desire attraction?

I even talk to the Malabar vines wilted
around a broken violin under my writing desk.

I talk bright & constantly in my yard.

The bright & the constant distinctly align
with Polaris during late night walks.

Sometimes we follow our instincts
as much as we desire facts.

Don't we crave staring at the horizon
as much as we long to hover?

Can you teach me the illusion of holding still?
Can you teach my malignant masses

nestled against my uterine walls
how not to heart-attack?

or at least how not to fear the flight?

The Labor of Counterpoint
after J.S.Bach

The last movement
of Johann Sebastian Bach's *Concerto*

for Two Violins, Strings and Continuo
works for memorizing the center of d minor.

It is good for identifying the sound
before the noun like she inside the shears.

It is good for throat clearing another's larynx
almost like the wrangling of course tresses.

It works for stippling gestures or shaving
the bottoms of hairs curling in

before Getting Ready.
Bravery. I feel

God. O I feel good for pushing
out small fires, fanning that fan's fan

from alerts forming any higher inside the body,
in from the sleights as if Saturn devoured

ventricles into vengeance—but Bach works
for understanding this as counterpoint, counterclaims,

and for those contrarians—it's good
for the sacred secular and for second opinions.

This is good for Getting Ready.
Bravery

or interning each other's specked eye,
for locking gazes across a dressing gown

for unclasping the speculum, for entering
each other's stairways and adjustments of spines.

Ways to subvert.
Ways of the breath.

Ways of the mouth.
Slipping under the lingering

weighs beyond the coursing

Getting Ready.
Bravery.

Hot and flashing, hands to neck,
clavicle to shoulders, right to mid,

intravenous to tense, left to lowered,
rift to driftwood, drift to pain

O Conversion O Convulsing
thighs fanning as the fan

spins out—and Bach's not even pentatonic.
This mode is good for interlocking,

like an Operatic trill
holding its metallic turn,

downside & for the Opening.
Oh, that Opening—

Hum, Burn, Sun.

O layers of the Land and Sea.
Help Me.

Unsound Health

after "Comptine d'un autre ete, l'apre" by Yann Tiersen

When walking on a boardwalk that enters a park named *Anxiety*,

or the woodsiest wood of the woods, my beloved then asks, *can we talk?*

But maybe he's thinking about naturalness versus human-made

or about the passing jive that moves through this part of the Paumanok,

on this hidden sandbar, on this long walk, into these woodsy woods of wood.

Maybe he's concerned about the wild turkey pluralizing the geese,

wondering whether we should cross over into dangerous blue-green algae.

Now we are semi-running, but still not really talking about the risk

into these woodsy woods of darkening coo or reminiscent of heaven,

as them turkeys following us, shaking their bulky tail feathers,

necks, and heads as if they swallowed the scold of their indexes.

Their presence is perfect for spoiling the mood,

      for saying Keep Out but Love Me Anyhow, especially

      when watching your love stride ahead almost half a mile,

      as you fall further back, wanting the disrespect to turn into a hex.

Fractures

In Madrid
I was on my way to a market I think with—

when Mary said
I looked lost again

Isn't it funny how the body continues to press
for water even when there is little left—

Mary said
I looked like I lost weight—

I mentioned that I broke my rosary beads
on cobblestone in Montreal—

Mary asked
if I meant Madrid—

I thought I said I was on my way
through a market on a cobblestone street
when I fell

Mary asked me
if I'm okay—

Isn't it funny how the humidity
strips what's already weak—

Mary half-agreed—

when my eyes welled up
into an aisle of stone, she confirmed

this pain as a Blessing—

She reminded me
how it takes a very special person
to leave you injured in a foreign place—

A Quiet Surge of Dystopia

Your body became a retainer for stress, often pulled between affording fuel or fast food off a greasy dollar menu. You thought about taking up a fourth job as your friends suggested you work with them at a public interest research group for whom they would go door-to-door letting people know about possible toxins in their water supply and ways they could get involved or sign petitions for local climate concerns. But when you would meet up with them at coffee shops and dive bars, although they made some leeway, they vented their frustrations about how people wouldn't open their doors or how they would be yelled at or chased off properties. These stories made you reconsider applying for the job. You imagined walking miles through neighborhoods begging people from different backgrounds than yours to heed your environmental doomsday warnings.

On the Snowy Shore of Lake Erie

My date brought torn Wonder Bread for the gulls
and when he aired Basho's haiku, the birds
went missing, except for a few feathers down

spinning from the swift movements of a brown-
striped osprey maneuvering high above us & when we
searched the barren parking lot for the nestlings,

he brought us plastic Solo cups for boxed wine,
before offering me candy. After watching him
oust the crumbs from his beard, the showgirl

in me turned to new frequencies, tempered
like how my grandmother insisted I try *again*
the Jamaican sorrel I named sour. And so,

I read him a few Wendell Berry poems until
we acted tired by the expiring light or until
we could no longer feel the stretched miles

sheepish at the splint edges of each other's blunt
stares or until we finally sampled the other's upper-
core against the frozen sand on a white-knuckled

hill reshaped like the wing of a black-veined butterfly,

& when blood stopped inside a cave in his face,

& for no reason holy, evidence of connectedness

laid a supine body over mine and what came

heaving was starving in so many directions.

Still Life & Half-Turned Lover

after Nicky Beer

First the artist painted greys of the Great South Bay

before spreading sand erosion off Tobay Beach.

Then he blotted thousands of pebbles under

an old catamaran and two helmet crabs

tossed among the sparse grassland.

Above them, he imploded stars for hours—

the hues withdrew from their shine

as the murky outlines of naked bathers waned.

When the artist set down his brushes, on cue

the lover repositioned the easel to the back corner

—out of view—

near her sketch of N.C. Wyeth's *The Hunter*.

After an hour of woolgathering in separate rooms,

they returned for whiskey then sexed position to position.

The artist fell asleep before the lover
whose semi-insomnia endured a hailstorm

of questions provoking the difference
between a tornado warning and a watch.

Will the gale protest these walls too much?
she pondered.

Eventually, the lover wandered barefoot
into the unlit kitchen, still boozy

with fumes of oil paints. In the dark,
she took a peeling knife to a navel's rind.

Such tension loosened her tongue
like the fraying end of a relationship.

On the Last Day of Becoming Us
for O

We were dead thistles
but we pinched back.

We were warped
but we were barbed.

We had playtime
but spangled blood.

We followed an eviction
but I'll admit, I was afraid.

We were internal wars
but plucked guitars.

So, what if we broke
soft bones from yield signs?

We were dirty nail beds
swabbed with moonshine.

We were matted water
but lumbered tongues.

Isn't this romantic?
We were grown here

like invasive cathedrals.
We ripped up

Rembrandt's light
last seen in our photos.

We were chapel ceilings
of indolent beliefs.

We were crucifixes lost
between breasts.

We hunted for heaven
by pretending

we were centipedes
hiding in pillow shams.

Even if we did not admit
our exposed nerves,

we both knew deep
into the proximity

of suffering alone, we
were glory thieves

for each other's power.

A Field Guide for a Positive Mental Attitude

When you drive on past your childhood home,
try not to overanalyze the improvements as a setback.

Although ignition coils are decades old,
accelerate up the dirt road with swerve and intention.

A field of delphiniums is worth the wear and tear
when recalling how your lover relaxed
into a coffin as if it were a hammock.

Reread his last letters from Kathmandu.

Repeat, *I can bear this.*

Learn to respect that silence rarely means *at rest.*

When you see how an egret returns to the capillary waves
replay the opening scene of your screenplay you will never write.

At every check engine warning,
wipe away the smear in the rearview mirror.

For any flat tire, fold your midi dress above the knees.

Kneel.

Repeat, *I can bear this.*

When you cannot loosen the lug nuts, stand as iron on iron.
Recite, *they who rise from the misty Cliffs of Moher*
and then try AAA again.

If you must fold your anxiety into sleep

then it's okay to take a back seat.

When your dead lover taps the middle of your forehead,
retrieve the image of two Buddhist monks & two barnacle geese
diverging on a dissected path.

Stare through cracked slots at what's no longer coupling with dusk.

When mosquitoes enter as misquotes at stage right, it's time to walk for help.

Repeat, *I will grin and bear this*
then hum.

Follow the panicles of creeping phlox
and the yellow shine under the power lines.

Give gratitude to the distillation of a hinterland
that won't let go of water weight.

But when it does, and the rain gathers on the road,
and the disarray of debris rakes your sandals,
blame infrastructure and not mother nature.

Repeat, *I can bear this. I can bear this* even when
you can only think of how you cannot bear children.

Repeat, *I cannot bear children* until you can no longer discern vanity.

Like a single-cell thunderstorm, reproductive death
is rarely graceful despite its grace.

Over airbuds listen to anything Rachmaninoff for stressing deep
endings of strings, trumpeters, timpanists, & glorifiers.

Memorize the tonal distinctions between
the untimely rumblings of hunger & instinct.

Patience holds reasonable promise in the clench of its jawline.

Let your throat's pain repeat,

this body is full of silent alarms.

A Quiet Surge of Dystopia

Oddly enough, negligent landlords had prepared you well for Superstorm Sandy, which arrived in October 2012. You already had no hot water and a dead refrigerator used for over-sized textbooks. In anticipation of the storm, your landlord had fastened plywood over the only 2x4 ft window in the room, which had a gap between the glass pane and the frame, typically letting in an ecosystem of insects and rainwater that ran like a sitcom you no longer found humorous.

Me and Monster

Our Good Morning mantra is What You See is What You Get.

We like to scrutinize the scrutinizing God as a superlative act
during meditation.

We sing about hair suicides in the shower. Ain't Dat a Shame.
God, Stop Her. Sink Stopper. Garbage Dispose of Her.

We don't watch our stress or blood pressure levels.

We eat quackery beliefs, allergies Our Daily Wheat Gluten, Corn Syrup,
Glyph this & that, BHT, Yellow No. 5 & 6 - 7 - 8 chemicals,
to name a few in our rotten stew.

We make appeaser people-pleasers
& give away elderspeak that smells like gold.

We hunt for drama. We stare at those who ignore history.
We boo-hiss against their teeth if we have too.

But we hide when we get suckered or be thrown back
in the rodeo or when we work with vices in woodshop.

If we had a dollar for every time we've been asked at a bar-be-cue
to spoon in a bed, in a bar, in a video, on the streets, on the beach,

or with questions that subjugate hate,
we could buy matching neck plates.

We have kissed toads & rattlesnakes.
We've worn leather & serpent ferns & socks full of money to burn.

We even make up words in our texturized frames
& like autocorrect asterisks, we like to shake our bare breasts.

But we hide 'misunderstandings' in our corsets.
Sometimes we'd rather wear our masks than open our oxygen.

I do not like to practice judgements, except at night. Me and Monster
make up games of windfall as we lick our ice cream gavels,

& before we sleep in our sweat, we yowl as mooncalves,
then trap each other's prayers in our overgrown cares.

A Quiet Surge of Dystopia

After reading Scott Bryson's essay "Between the Earth and Silence," you wondered if the project of most contemporary ecopoets does "fall somewhere between two objectives: to know the world and to recognize its ultimate unknowability." So, as you prepared for Sandy's landfall, you tried your best not to see "her" superiority as an enemy, but as a natural phenomenon that would soon exist in the same space as you. You headed to the market, bought two bunches of bananas, three avocados, limes, whatever beverages were left on the shelf after water had sold out, Roma tomatoes, flour tortillas, two jars of peanut butter, a box of Cheerios, boxed soy milk, a couple of saint candles, a Bic lighter.

After Superstorm Sandy came and left, you weathered the blackout by rearranging parts of your room, reading Louis Simpson, writing poems, rising and settling in with the sun. You considered the two-week break from digital technology a sort of welcomed reprieve and unplanned meditation on self-reliance, at least until you read that over a hundred people died in the storm. You kept the door to the outside open for light and wore your winter coat too. You used your car as a phone charger to text your mother because you couldn't call out. A week later when the food ran out, still without electricity, you walked cautiously through a mile of power lines downed by trees to the market again, which had no generator and was rank with rotting meats and rotten fruit. It was a surreal harvest. The disfigured aisles tested depth perception in an apocalyptic scene the size of a small auditorium, eerily devoid of elevator music.

Directions for Singing

after John Wesley

Sing whatever makes you think
we enjoyed being led to a flood zone.

Sigh if you must, for a conscience
does not drown quickly in a bird fight.

Although it might take forever to untether,
think of yourself risen from a dredging machine.

Lift others as if you are not ashamed
of being hurt. Have an eye out for beekeepers.

Do not be afraid of modesty, or be afraid
to bawl in front of the congregation.

If it's a crossroad for you, walk the false alley
like it's a blessing or amplify your guttural tones.

And when you see yourself drenched in a public
bathroom mirror, strive your voice with the faucet's

hammer. Hum with the offhandedness of overcast,
or until you drive the refractory storm clouds out.

A Quiet Surge of Dystopia

Concerned about proper climate control, the father of two children you taught music lessons had asked before Superstorm Sandy which floor of their split-level ranch he should station their upright piano. You didn't realize until after the superstorm that your answer to place it upstairs would save its life. This family lived in the Village of Lindenhurst, known for linden trees. His two-story ranch house was among the many one-story bungalows off the Great South Bay canals. They were told to evacuate beforehand, and although officially warned to take shelter at a local gymnasium, he chose to hunker and keep the family and pets at home to wait it out. They often received storm warnings in the past that had come to no fruition. But Sandy's seven-foot storm surge swept matter-of-factly through their backyard fence and the first floor of their home, continuing for miles toward the main street. An unwelcomed river swarmed their home as they held up on the second floor. He later relayed how lucky his family was to keep their house after officials had condemned so many one-story houses to demolition. If they hadn't the advantage of a family member who owned a mold remediation business, it may not have been the case. But in the snowy days after Sandy, as the waters drained, their small pets died from the cold, and the father would tell you later how every time it rained his children would panic.

Bonefish

At my birthday dinner,
I chose the woodstove salmon,
despite my ex-love dictating
from a parasitic medical book,
in his blood-stained scrubs,
the ways uncooked saltfish
could infest the stomach
lining with tapeworm.
Even when I silenced myself,
blinking wildly away
our intestinal tubing,
his Russian dialect
continued whispering bright
light through the back-
door of my black hair.

This took me from the present,
and I wanted to be present.

I wanted to eat the woodstove salmon

I did not want to pretend
someone didn't kick through walls
as I looked down again
at my very own plate
of my girl grilled
in her pink guts, as if to say:

It's *Game Over, hominid*—

even when I could
scale this into a slendro
and instead say: It's *Gamelan, honey.*
When will I understand
about why *gongs* were going off
on Indigenous islands?
During my undergraduate years
I knew I should have gone
to the library's card-catalog
researching instead of memorizing
only the words *bonang* & *wayang.*

So, when the waiter asked:
Ma'am, is everything okay?
How's the salmon?
I kept thinking
how knowing better
has me in a chokehold,
as if burying another's bones
was my birthright.

Instead, when the waiter asked,
Ma'am, how is everything?
I stuck a fork in it
and showed my teeth
as nature has taught me
when holding a knife to its neck,
saying: *It's fine—It's all fine.*

The Limitations of Repose

I often discourage undergraduate students from overusing the words *happy* or *sad* in their personal essays in the same way my mother would remind me how my habit of answering "It's fine"was bland and lacked personality.

And even when I thought to insist "but it *is* fine, "I wondered if "it" was meant for "I"?

Why are you without a Home?
for N

You have been given questions to which you cannot be given answers.
–Wendell Berry

where's your haunt? your hearsay? your hector?
your heckler? your harasser? your hysteria? your "hive"?

are we talking about carpenter bees or colonies?

why do you keep hankering?
do you want a hawthorn or a hyacinth?
pollen or a poison?

or are you talking about we or me?

where's your house? your holdup? your handout? your hitchhike?
your hallucination? your hologram? your happy meal? your holiday?

where's my holy ground?

who clamors about your hipbone?
or theorizes about your hymen?

is this conversation even hygienic?

why skip inside the hippocampus?
why loop inside the hippocampus?

why do we continue to hula-hoop?

and how are your headaches?

before or after the hysterectomy?

Ascending from a Slough

this brain hears
this brain is a noun
     like a slough
     unsafe town
this brain bitches
     in the matrix
     noticing new age marks
     like staged art
this brain recalls plays on repeat
     Maroon lineage
     cinchona and juniper trees
     wild berries and vines
this brain curls and twists hair
     thinks that right braids left
this brain breaks off roots
this brain lunches
     says hello to other brains
     gives gratitude
     receives thanks
     sometimes ignored
this brain sometimes accused of theft
     sometimes makes accusations
     but dislikes intervening
     although acknowledges but
     doesn't recognize
     species under cognizable means
this brain drinks with considerations
recalls plays and repeats
     confirmations and generalizations

then identifies specializations or tries
its hands at productions
this brain's motivations
    trumps and trashes
    can also be aristocratic and dogmatic
    sometimes rolls with the homies
    sometimes rolls glass marbles
    with relativism and nihilism
    wears empires and grey matters
    tooth molds and foot fungus
    sometimes loses sight and hearing
    isn't and doesn't but has in the past
this brain echoes
this brain's confinement often indicates
    fluttering in the honeyguide
    gauges and tailgates
    stops at green lights
    disrobes through stop signs
    ligaments overstretched
    like contraceptives
this brain classifies colors and names
    remembers hand-breaking
    through the webbed jungles after
    the left knee scraped open
this brain sees red lights
    riding through Mount Diablo
    discovering colonial schoolhouses
    abandoned into the gully of St. Mary
this brain remembering Ochi's Limestone
    curls its toes onto the Dunn's River
    glances down at the sea of people
    pressed against a vertical drop

this brain thinks it's going to cascade
      thinks about the dying
this brain skanks against heat
      spiders but does not howl
      like certain wolves
the brain returns to *good woman* as medicinal
      reads *Hip Logic* as hierophantic
      repeats jazz playlists
      like modes of mixolydian
      repeats Keith Jarrett
      scaling pianos like cymbals
this brain deconstructs political
      definitions into refined sugars
      then crashes
this brain thinks of its open gap
      drooling bacterium
      recalls 1986
      reboots Chernobyl
      and a pen pal among the nuclear
      who wanted freedom
      who wanted to escape
      who wanted useful answers
      who wants better policies
      who wants a finer sleep package
this brain wants an extraterrestrial
      rhetorical moral DNA
but this brain recycles
      uncomfortable dialogues
wants to refurbish its brand
      as a hybrid
      as recycled like how

this brain's biological guilt
      wakes the gut in the middle of this REM cycle
      hums a few notes about losing religion
      claims they're marriage material but
this brain knows brains short out
      combust or break down as compost
      sees dead insects as dead keepsakes
      discovers dragonflies aren't the only cannibals
      as it eats slaughtered animals
but this brain believes there are in fact incompatible economies
this brain
      can't help to see
      anything but

A Quiet Surge of Dystopia

You attended a monthly poetry reading that took place in one of the tiniest, oldest stained-glass churches across a pond, which often floods the streets in heavy rain. During an intermission, a local church historian shared that a devout member of the congregation, named "Bessie," used to arrive at Sunday services by rowboat.

Rowboat?

You didn't know how to swim. You were afraid of the water. Your mind buzzed with wilderness, inundated by images of your sunken electrical piano and *you* drowning through your floating possessions.

To the Eyes Beholding Stardust

Whether or not you are part of my ancestral Seas: from the North,
Irish & Caribbean — it's not pretty trying to recall or forget the sale

of names — in borders & reports — about those who drowned, or swam
around screaming out, or those who took stamps, or those crimped,

attuning atop & below the salt water, and for those who lived,
where defeat railed as motors back to a "Heaven." Maybe

God was working on imitation & intimidation Here
leading to resistance, like how music doesn't really distract

from the back's burnout during plantation, harvest, & reconstruction.
But Here, we are still, recalling & forgetting, enslaved in noise

as stilted yellers, sellers, buyers, surveyors & researchers.
To my Fathers who are missing like the native ecology in the marina—

To my Mothers who ebb and rise like plastics—I'm sorry.
Why are we most troubled & so troublesome?

A Quiet Surge of Dystopia

You called your mom to complain about having to throw away favorite books that had grown mold from the encroaching moisture. She jokingly warned you from her safe retirement condo in Mesquite, Nevada that the "Island" you love is slowly going under—and how you should move nearer to her. You wondered if perhaps your wise mother was correct. Or was she only parroting rumors? You half laughed about this comment as if it were hyperbole, but then you recalled how a poet said, "Nature is not a caring mother addressed solely to our needs; the Earth has no perception of us as we see ourselves and our needs."

Spoke the Ancestral

Even if the others judge us as arbitrary,

out of line, on our knees in passages undetected by light

or as reborn, the elders say we should continually escape

to the green manurance. They say we

are not segregated from small-scale mining lungs

as they cough the blood dust into their handkerchiefs.

They say we must stop browbeating for copper & nickel.

We are not detouring metals. We become byproducts,

swallowing urgency like workhorses.

Even if we forgive conditions of the stench, the elders

recite proverbs through the dead macaw-feathers

as I sharpen my pencil on their machetes.

They say, *Prepare for Trials*, while uttering, *wat a bangarang*

as we pound out the *stinking toe fruit*.

When we harvest the sweet clusters

off the Guinep trees and no longer gossip

about sensational people, we stand quiet and listen.

They teach me how to clean Maccaback for fish tea

and mention how the pinking of my eyes

emanates from the garbage fires miles away.

I don't want to admit I like learning my ancestral stories

through trails of ash. It took decades, but even

the soot, the rats, the lizards and the roaches

sometimes embrace my grandmother's aging home.

The memory of her laugh rarely leaves her bedroom—

but my elders remind me how the bluest dreams

can harden into Streamertails like how reincarnation moves in two directions.

They shower me with reminders *to give no allegiance*

to any masters regardless of any person's position,

especially if they despise us *falling back into our poetic ears*

& despite the furthering *distance from our native clime.*

Dada
    for R

my grandfather
he is he is he is
facebook posts
wearing a dead face
eyeing me shy behind
his thick black frames
no matter where we stand
an american an african
a panamanian an irish-scot
jamaican spinning ices
under a metal veranda
where i have not visited
in the longest look
at his quiet face a repertory
of reversions an avid reader
like how i imagine a clockmaker
binging delicately about small
inspections of allspice
popping tropical collars
from under a sweater
before heading to work
at a d&g red stripe factory
for decades and for decades after
making his only trip to paris—

can we have a postcard of silence—

for he is he is he is
now a confined box
now a portraiture savoring
goat's cartilage until
crumbled into an odyssey

of who who who
might like like dislike me
cringing about this that
or how i wish i knew
my real grandfather's face
declaring to his *daughta*
how her daughter would be
an artist mourning us all
as if we awoke as animals
violated of privacy or private parts
that's now gone into a madhouse
that's sometimes not saying anything but
scattering into an almost shame
shame for not navigating back home

A Quiet Surge of Dystopia

Suppose this Island, whose roads flood often, was not landscaped with an entire ecology, or timeline, in mind. Suppose we are making our modifications primarily according to our prescribed aesthetic sense of beauty, while lacking consideration for the long-term sustainability of the design. The Long Island Sound, the Great South Bay and Atlantic Ocean might be on a mission to reclaim their space—and our lives as we know them along with it. You wonder if in your lifetime we would be forced to adapt.

Self-Portrait as a Bilateral Night

The rule is: there are no rules
-Shonda Rhimes

When my dentist notices I grind my teeth

I imagine how my heart must

punch through the mess of a hoarder's mind.

This morning, I noticed in the shower

bruises on my knees & rug burns

on my elbows again although

the thought of ash burr stings,

it shifts like petals of woodruff,

sweet aster or yarrow modified

away from their reproductive parts.

And when I stop talking to myself,

the Goodnight texts back that he misses

me too like in a tune of a bland compliment

or stress relief for a mistress,

but then again, I am not,

so why do I dismiss the *we*?

When we meet for after-hours
why do I field-mark embarrassment
through the language of bird meat
when I have no appetite?

Last week, after sex, I answered
that I was the first among my siblings.

Why have I been seen as secondary?
Doesn't love exists for the first line of defense
was my second to last thought above ground

on a westbound rail with no one
around but that which lulled me
into a study of discontentment:

Look there. A mosaic of a lily pad on a subway wall,
pixelated green, faking freedom, bodice like a padlock,
while a sparrow imitates a dragon kite.

Our Quarantine Story
after Dorothea Grossman / Aimee Nezhukumatathil

During the pandemic, after my fiancé was laid off, it was his idea
to forage for edible weeds around Queens when our food grew scarce.

From the stoop, I would watch him crouched on one knee,
his bare hands between telephone poles,

pulling up green stars from the control joints
under our mailbox full of clover mites & commercial flyers.

I almost forgot how sprawl could be so quiet.

When he returned inside, he rinsed off the stalks,
placed a rolled lot on his tongue and then on mine.

He mentioned how "sticky" foods could be a delicacy
in other cultures, as I turned my back and coughed them out.

And later in the evening, he read to me about how
Indigenous women prevented pregnancy by drinking

cleaver tea, as he handed me a tall cup of it swirling with clover honey.

A Warning about Entanglements

When I mention that I no longer crave
coupledom, the hostess finger-snaps

for the *Peach Bellini* the bartender *just made*,
and like a vexed fox pulled from its den,

I press apart worry as the head server
recites the arrangement of species as *Specials*.

This might be what it was to die. As she emphasizes
the pan-seared rainbow trout with its skin still on,

the grizzly inside me self-reflecting
at the riverbank did not want to bite it out.

The Lovers Move to the Pine Barrens

Down-and-Out often nestle
hand-in-hand like two lone star ticks
found buried above the sternum.

Watch them trance.
Watch them yawn
wilderness into a night's surge.

Often, Down-and-Out transmit
their anesthetic touch to the other,
deciding not to harbor children.

Watch them head-trip. Watch
them overthink *themselves single*
as strobes through the pinelands

while gorging through soil gullies
of tar stumps and vanishing squawks.
Watch them logging concerns.

Watch them split as they release
cares about the rocky beaches'
former self. The glacial physique.

When Down-and-Out exchange

vows sub-secretly, like the mid stage

of Lyme disease, watch them

toggle in sickness and in needing help.

Watch them uproot a bright repeat.

Freedom from Fear
after Shostakovich

The ostinato movement of Shostakovich's
Piano Trio No. 2 works for staring at his picture
taped above my headboard
like the oasis of a father safely home every night.
It's good for remembering your kin
crawling in scores under floorboards,
under ships wrecked, and in and out of bureau drawers.
This teaches me about bravery.
This teaches me about the violence of haste.
Is Thou art marking a bull's eye egotistical?
I cannot barely write words efficiently
above the ground with clean water
and mechanical pens. Still, the trio runs
good for how we glower and worry
about fascists and Nazis.
This trains me about my homeland, this island's idleness,
as I watch out for boats breaching the shorelines.
It reminds me of what's set to livid,
trying to disown me from my brown heritage.
I often ask myself for a truth about the eyes, how
mine are not that different from yours. Have we adjusted
the ownership of the word dark?
This teaches me that dark isn't a color or even human.
It's good for the glorified boldface lie,
for the claw-grip, but without hurry
as it strokes the upper tips of our ears,
ever more, ever slight, or an ever stinging
like you and I are animals in training,

like you and I are animals in separate cages.
This is good for beyond the bedridden brambles.
This teaches beyond me, how the coffin
relates to the night's music.

A Quiet Surge of Dystopia

Every year you watched the same local news reports about how young professionals were moving away from the island. You marveled at the million-dollar homes continuing to be built when so many hard-working people were unable to afford living expenses. You frequented online housing forums and saw many people seeking to give up their houses with multiple bedrooms in favor of living in tiny houses hoping they wouldn't have to pay high property taxes, so they could save enough for retirement, so they could enjoy simpler and healthier lives. You began asking if it was possible for people to come together in order to buy land collectively. Many others who were far from qualifying for a mortgage on their own were forced to reside in cramped spaces with multiple roommates. Could young artists and professionals work together as a community to create farms based on permaculture design principles, which prioritize care of the earth and of people over profit? For the first time, you wondered if the problems could be the solutions. Could industrial waste be a resource or greenhouse gasses be fuel? Could money be put aside because food grows on trees? Could the encroaching waters rotate turbines to create electricity? As in any great musical composition, or formal poem, or pattern of any storm or system in nature, could the slowly building tension inside you be leading to release? Could the festering sensation that something was terribly wrong finally become a realization that there could be a better way of life? That you could have it and deserve it?

how to cradle a stranger

when you embrace her, hold her neck & shoulders in the hook of your arm.
if her eyes remain open, slow-dance inside her irises or soften into her soft
whites. if her eyes start to close, quietly repeat her name. if you must apply
pressure to arteries, think of your little sister concentrating on solitaire,
or imagine your firstborn creating snow angels, or consider blackberry stains
on the concrete sidewalk as part of a lost paradise. blood is blood.
careful not to move her. you cannot judge a torqued form by how it retreats
or when it collapses into the unconscious. when your embrace numbs
your body, try not to chew away the inside of your cheek. planetary grief
is planetary grief. instead, hold her as she is someone's child. quietly
say her name. and when there's no answer: because there are no answers:
repeat | repeat | repeat.

Dear Power, We Possess

We, the field workers, have no memory of Adam & Everafter. /
We did not choose / from the Great Tree or chartered dichotomies /
this waitlist for help. / Many of us were taught by oral stories or a Great Book, /
that We were rustled up as grub dust and a dry rib, / but /
We no longer understand the encroachment of metropolitan unrest. /
So, how long must we wait for help? / We, the field workers,
surrounded by danger / unending warring /on a weekly basis /
stand reminded / this might be a test. /
We cannot find this option of being healed by Your Light /
or the light of missiles /*So, how long must we wait for help?* /
Do you understand that We no longer understand the field? /
We, the fallen / the apple / the pomegranate / the avocado /
the mango / the fig / the olive / the black mulberries. / Starve. /
We, the arroyo, wait. /
So, how long must we wait for help? /
We, the hunters, the finger-tracers, the skins' makers of fragileness. /
We, the appearance & disappearance of the volcanic, / breathe ash. /
So, how long must we wait for help? / We offer You as We offered you
our restless / as we must gather more witnesses, /
So, how long must we wait for help? /

Notes

"Opening" was written to my most favorite Philip Glass' "Opening."

"Me and Monster" is after Thylias Moss's "An Anointing."

"Still Life & Half-Turned Lover" is inspired from the title by Nikki Bear.

"The Lovers in the Pine Barrens" borrows a phrase "bright repeat" from Melissa Hunter Gurney.

"Unsound Health" was written to the music composition "Comptine d'un autre ete, l'apre" by Yann Tiersen from the film *Amelie*.

"Partial Life Review" borrows transitional phrases from Marie Howe's "Part of Eve's Discussion."

"The Labor of Counterpoint " was written to J.S. Bach's Double Violin Concerto in D minor, Mvt.

"Strange & Merciful Days" contains a small segment commissioned by NYFA artist series—a small erasure from Sylvia Plath's poem "Mad Girl's Love Song."

"A Field Guide for a Positive Mental Attitude" was inspired by Napoleon Hill's advice on developing a positive mind set.

"Directions for Singing" borrows the title and form after John Wesley.

In "In Preparation for Ascendance (1993)," higglers are Jamaican vendors who work the outside markets. Pickney means "kid" in Jamaican Patois/Patwah.

A *wha do dem man yah, Cha!* is roughly translated to "What are you going to do with these men, Cha?" in Jamaican Patois/Patwah. *men dem* translated to "men" in Jamaican Patois/Patwah.

"Freedom from Fear" was written to Dimitri Shostakovich's Piano Trio No. 2 in E minor, Mvt II.

"how to cradle a stranger" is in memory of Breonna Taylor.

"Spoke the Ancestral" borrows italicized phrases from Claude McKay's *Harlem Shadows*.

"A Quiet Surge of Dystopia (Nature is not a caring mother...)" includes an Ed Roberson's quote taken from the anthology *Black Nature*.

Thank You

Super grateful for the support of my mom [June], Brigit, and loving family and grandparents.

Thank you for the invaluable care, advice, joy, and patience in helping me through versions of this collection—line by line, word by word: Carrie Addington, Jennifer Franklin, Terrance Hayes, Craig Kite, Patricia Smith/VCFA workshop, Dan Chaisson's, Aimee Nezhukumatathil's, and Jennifer Grotz's Bread Loaf Environmental Writing Poetry Workshops.

And super special thanks to my wonderfully wise lifesavers, my university and writing mentors [and friends], especially Gene Hammond, Julie Sheehan, Roger Thompson, Peter Khost, and Tracey Walters.
I am beholden to such beautiful spirits and guidance: Rashmi Rai & family, Molly Gaudry, Star Black, Robert Kaplan, Melissa Hunter Gurney, Ama Codjoe, Tara Propper-Kelly, Shane and Maddie O'Hanlon, Annemarie Waugh, Joe Labriola, Richard Bronson, Rev. Frank, MaryAnn Duffy, Maya Washington, and Carrie Addington for lovingly holding space when grief and illness quietly took me over and down. I will always hold the memory of your radiant light with me.

I extend gratitude to my loving friends who lifted spirits and also artists whose work and/or words are an inspiration: Sarah Azzara, Shirine Babb, Yvonne Bendzlowicz, Wandra Chenault, Suzannah Gail Collins, Sergio Ariel Gomez Diaz, Jess F, Ross Gay, Philip Glass, Russ Green, Sarah Green, Sarah Gutowski, Yona Harvey, francine j. harris, Major Jackson, Katherine Johnston, Donika Kelly, Kristina Lucenko, John Marshall "tysm," Jilleen May, Matthew Miranda, Shara McCallum, McCrann Family, Dr. Melissa Nicosia, Rebecca Hart Olander, Jane Ormerod, Martha Rhodes, Frances Richey, Henk Roussow, Alan Semerdjian, Otar Taktakishvili, David Taylor, Lou Ann Walker, George Wallace, and Alexandra Van de Kamp.

Thank you to Kristina Marie Darling for your steadfast advice, editing help, hard work, and discernment with this collection. And I extend gratitude to

Erin Elizabeth Smith and Sundress Publications for their generosity and time on this project.

About the Author

Michelle Whittaker is an American poet of West Indian heritage and the author of *Surge*, which was awarded a Next Generation Indie Book Award [great weather for MEDIA, 2017]. She has been published in *The New York Times Magazine*, *The New Yorker*, *Shenandoah*, *Gulf Coast*, The Academy of American Poets' Poem-a-Day series, and other publications. She has received a Pushcart Special Mention, a Cave Canem Fellowship, and a NYFA Fellowship in Poetry. She is an Associate Professor in Creative / Expository Writing in the Program in Writing and Rhetoric at Stony Brook University.

Other Sundress Titles

DANGEROUS BODIES/ANGER ODES
stevie redwood
$16

Back to Alabama
Valerie A. Smith
$16

Grief Slut
Evelyn Berry
$16

Ruin & Want
José Angel Araguz
$20

Age of Forgiveness
Caleb Curtiss
$16

Where My Umbilical is Buried
Amanda Galvan-Huynh
$16

In Stories We Thunder
V. Ruiz
$16

Slack Tongue City
Mackenzie Berry
$16

Good Son
Kyle Liang
$16

Slaughterhouse for Old Wives Tales
Hannah V Warren
$16

Nocturne in Joy
Tatiana Johnson-Boria
$16

Another Word for Hunger
Heather Bartlett
$16

Little Houses
Athena Nassar
$16

the Colored page
Matthew E. Henry
$16

Year of the Unicorn Kidz
jason b. Crawford
$16

www.ingramcontent.com/pod-product-compliance
Lightning Source LLC
Chambersburg PA
CBHW031146090426
42738CB00008B/1243